Looking at...
ALCOHOL

Julie Johnson

WAYLAND

First published in 2009 by Wayland

Copyright © Wayland 2009

Wayland
338 Euston Road
London NW1 3BH

Wayland Australia
Level 17/207 Kent Street
Sydney NSW 2000

Produced for Wayland by
White-Thomson Publishing Ltd

+44 (0) 845 362 8240
www.wtpub.co.uk

Editors: Sonya Newland and Katie Powell
Designer: Robert Walster

British Library Cataloguing in Publication Data
Johnson, Julie
Looking at alcohol
   1. Drinking of alcoholic beverages - Juvenile literature
   2. Alcoholism - Juvenile literature
   I. Title II. Alcohol
   362.2'92

ISBN: 9780750259040

Picture Credits

Allsport: 45; Bridgeman Art Library: 12; Camera Press: 22; Cephas: *title page*, 8, 41; Corbis: *cover* (Martin Ruetschi/Keystone), 15 (Ashley Cooper), 26 (Gero Breloer/epa); Dreamstime: 14 (Nounstudio), 42 (Sireagle); Getty Images: 16 (Mary Evans Picture Library: 10; Eye Ubiquitous: 42 (Paul Seheult); Ronald Grant Archives: 31; Angela Hampton: 38; Robert Harding: 6 bottom, 27, 30; Hodder Wayland Picture Library: 11 top and bottom, 13, 17 (Gordon Clements), 20 (Tizzie Knowles), 28 (Howard J. Davies), 37 (Tizzie Knowles), 40; Impact: 4 (Alex MacNaughton), 9 (Steve Parry), 19 (Andy Johnstone), 23 (Alex MacNaughton), 25 (Andy Johnstone), 29 (Andy Johnstone), 36 (Bruce Stephens), 44 (Andy Johnstone); Panos: 18, 5 (Liba Taylor), 7 (Sean Sprague), 24 (Liba Taylor), 33 (Mark Schlossman), 35 (Clive Shirley); Popperfoto: 32, 39; Skyjold: 16 top; Topham Picturepoint: 34.

Printed in China

Wayland is a division of Hachette Children's Books, an Hachette UK company.
www.hachette.co.uk

Every attempt has been made to clear copyright. Should there be any inadvertent omission please apply to the publisher for rectification.

CONTENTS

What is alcohol?

If you asked most people if they take drugs they would say they do not. However, medicine, alcohol, cigarettes and even tea and coffee are all types of drugs, because they affect the mind and body in some way.

⬆ Social drinking is part of life for many people all over the world.

The effects of alcohol

Alcohol is a depressant drug because it slows down the body and makes people feel more confident. This might make someone slur their words, but it could make them more talkative.

FACT

Alcohol is often not thought of as a drug — largely because its use is common for both religious and social purposes in most parts of the world. It is a drug, however, and compulsive drinking in excess is one of modern society's most serious problems.

ADDICTION RESEARCH FOUNDATION, TORONTO, CANADA.

Why do people drink?

Although some types of drug are illegal, alcohol is legal and socially acceptable in most parts of the world. People drink alcohol for lots of different reasons. Some people use alcohol to help them relax at the end of a busy day, for example. Homeless people may drink alcohol to help them cope with having no job or home.

'I think that as long as you drink in moderation, alcohol is okay. It's when people go out and get drunk that the problems begin.'

SOPHIA, 16

⬇ A group of men enjoy a beer together in Mexico.

How is alcohol made?

Alcohol is a chemical called ethyl alcohol or ethanol. It can be made from most kinds of food, including fruit, grain and vegetables. Alcohol is made through processes called fermentation and distillation. How strong an alcoholic drink is depends on how it is made, and different drinks are made in different ways.

Making beer

Beer is usually made from hops or barley and water. Yeast is added to ferment the mixture.

⬇ Spirits, such as whisky, are distilled in large factories like this one in Scotland.

Making wine

Most wine is made from grapes. The grapes are crushed and the juice is mixed with yeast to make it ferment. Yeast changes the sugar in the grape juice into alcohol. Fortified wine is made stronger by adding another type of alcohol, such as brandy.

Making spirits

Spirits such as whisky, vodka, gin and rum are also made from grains, fruit and vegetables. Spirits are fermented and then distilled to make the alcohol stronger and purer. The spirit is then stored for between six months and several years to improve the taste.

⬆ These women are making beer, using a local recipe, in Tanzania, Africa.

FACT

Many different countries have their own traditional drink made from local produce. In Ireland, people drink *potcheen*, which is a strong spirit made from potatoes. In Jamaica there is a local gin made from bananas.

Types of alcohol

There are many different kinds of alcohol. These vary around the world depending on the ingredients available in that area. The main types of alcohol are:

• Beer (including lager, ale and stout).

• Wine (including white, rosé and red wine, and Champagne).

• Cider (made from apples or pears).

• Fortified wine (including sherry, port and vermouth).

• Spirits (including whisky, gin, vodka, brandy and rum).

• Liqueurs or flavoured spirits.

⬇ Different kinds of alcohol are lined up on a bar counter. Some are mixed with fruit juice or other drinks.

CASE STUDY ▸ CASE STUDY ▸ CASE STUDY ▸ CASE STUDY ▸

Jake first tried alcohol when he was on holiday when he was 14 years old. In the bars, the staff didn't ask how old Jake and his friends were, and they could buy any drink they liked. Jake usually drank lager, but then he decided to try spirits. After an hour, he began to feel dizzy. Later he was sick all over his friend. He had a terrible hangover the next day.

→ Many teenage boys drink lager and beer.

The strength of alcohol

Alcoholic drinks contain different amounts of pure alcohol. For example, beer and wine contain less pure alcohol than spirits or fortified wine.

Some alcohol, such as wine, is usually drunk on its own. Spirits are stronger than other types of alcohol and are usually mixed with a non-alcoholic drink called a mixer. Mixers make the spirit taste less strong and improve the flavour.

Alcohol past and present

People have been making and drinking alcohol for thousands of years. For example, the ancient Egyptians made beer as long ago as 2250 BC. Some ancient peoples even worshipped alcohol as a source of 'good'. The Romans had their own god of wine called Bacchus, and alcohol was an important part of many Roman celebrations.

⬆ Bacchus, the god of wine, was worshipped by the Romans.

FACT

In the early twentieth century, small amounts of alcohol were sometimes given to babies to calm them down. Up until quite recently, mothers gave their babies gripe water, which contains alcohol. They thought this would take away the discomfort of wind that babies have after feeding.

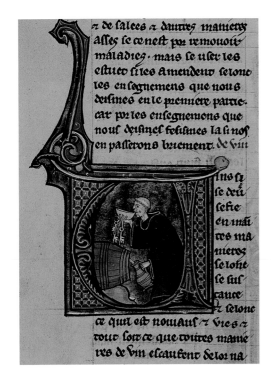

Alcohol as a medicine

In the past, people have used alcohol in a number of ways. Sometimes people who were very ill were given alcohol as a medicine. People who were feeling run-down drank alcohol as a tonic. For many years, wine was given to people to help them recover from a shock or illness. Spirits were even used to numb pain before doctors carried out operations such as setting broken bones.

⬆ Monks have made and drunk alcohol throughout their history. This monk is drinking ale.

⬇ This picture from 1823 shows people collecting and pressing apples to make cider.

Alcohol abuse

As time passed, more and more breweries and distilleries were established. As more alcoholic drinks were produced, drunkenness became an increasing problem.

⬆ This eighteenth-century painting shows drunken men in a club in London.

The barrel punishment

In sixteenth-century England, people who drank too much were 'dressed' in a beer barrel, with holes in the sides for their arms. They had to walk through the streets wearing the barrel.

Alcohol licences

By the eighteenth century, most countries had laws to try and limit drunken behaviour. Places that wanted to sell alcohol had to have a licence, for example. However, the consumption of alcohol continued to rise.

'Prohibition makes you want to cry into your beer and denies you the beer to cry into.'
DON MARQUIS, ARCHY AND MEHITABEL, 1927

Prohibition

In the 1920s, many countries – including the USA, Norway, Finland and Canada – banned alcohol completely. In the USA, this campaign against alcohol was called Prohibition. Laws were passed that made drinking alcohol illegal.

Despite the laws, people still found ways of getting hold of alcohol. Criminals called bootleggers made a lot of money by smuggling alcohol into secret drinking establishments. After much pressure from the American people, Prohibition ended in 1933.

⬅ During Prohibition in the USA, people still found ways of drinking alcohol. This woman is wearing a 'Rummy Apron' in which she could hide her drink.

The law and alcohol

Laws about drinking alcohol vary a great deal all over the world. There are laws about how old people can be before they can buy or drink alcohol. Other laws include where and when people are allowed to drink, and the amount of each kind of alcohol that can be sold.

'Why do they make such strong drinks if they are dangerous? I think they should only let people at bars and pubs have a limited amount of alcohol.'

JOANNA, 12, GLASGOW

Minimum-age laws

In most states in the USA, it is illegal for people to drink if they are under the age of 21. In Japan the minimum age is 20. In the UK and New Zealand, people can buy alcohol if they are over 18, but there is no law against drinking it at home at a younger age.

← Despite the minimum legal age for drinking, under-age drinking is an increasing problem in most countries.

↑ A British policeman does a breathalyser test on a driver.

Under-age drinking

In many countries there are still high numbers of under-age drinkers. It can be difficult for bar staff or shopkeepers to tell how old someone is, so people are often asked for identification to prove they are legally allowed to buy alcohol.

Drinking and driving

Most countries have also tried to crack down on drinking and driving. People who drink too much and then drive can be fined, banned from driving, or even put in prison.

Religion and alcohol

Each religion has a different view of drinking alcohol. Most religions allow some alcohol consumption, as long as it is drunk in moderation. However, some religions do not approve of any alcohol at all.

Christianity

Many Christians think that alcohol is acceptable as long as people are sensible about how much they drink. Although some Christian groups encourage their members not to drink at all, wine is used in Christian religious ceremonies. Priests use wine in the Mass to represent the blood of Christ.

⬆ Wine is part of the Christian Mass or Holy Communion service.

⬅ A Jewish family in Jerusalem stands for the blessing of the wine on Shabbat.

Judaism

Wine is also used in many Jewish ceremonies. One of these is Shabbat, which is celebrated every Friday night. At the beginning of the meal, the father raises a glass of wine, saying, 'Blessed is the name of the Lord, King of the Universe, who has given us the fruit of the vine'. Then everyone takes a sip of the wine.

'Keeping the body fit and healthy is part of serving God, for it is impossible to know and understand anything of the Creator's will if one is ill. Therefore a person should avoid anything that undermines bodily health.'
MAIMONIDIES (1135-1204), JEWISH PHILOSOPHER

Islam

In some Muslim countries, alcohol is completely forbidden. Strict Muslims will take great care not to come into any contact with alcohol. Giving or receiving it as a present is forbidden.

Sikhism

Sikhs are encouraged to keep a clear mind, and drinking is forbidden in Sikhism.

➡ In Pakistan, Muslim men socialize in teahouses where they drink tea, not alcohol.

What does alcohol do?

When we swallow alcohol, it goes first to the stomach, and is then carried round the body by the blood. It reaches all the organs, including the brain, and affects how people feel and behave.

'The first alcohol I tried was Champagne at a wedding. One glass made me feel all woozy.'

DIANA, 13

The effects of alcohol

After one or two drinks, people start to feel happy and relaxed. As they continue to drink, it becomes more difficult to do certain things, such as driving a car. Later, people may find it hard to talk and even to walk properly. If they continue drinking they will become very confused. They might collapse. They could even die from alcohol poisoning.

← One or two drinks can make people feel happy and carefree.

➡ Drinking a lot can make people do things they would not normally do, such as singing loudly and shouting.

THE SHORT-TERM EFFECTS OF ALCOHOL

Blood alcohol (mg/100ml)	Beer drunk (pints)	Effects on the mind and body
20	½-¾	Judgement is affected, tension is released, feel more carefree.
50	1½	Tension and stress of everyday life lessened. Driving performance affected.
60	2	Hand and arm movements affected, speech becomes clumsy. Driving affected badly.
80	2½-3	Begin to stagger, talk loudly, emotions are affected. Unsafe to drive.
100	3	Deeper areas of the brain affected, feel confused, may become sleepy.
160	5	May become aggressive. Memory loss is possible.
300	10	Difficult to arouse if asleep, not capable of voluntary action. Could lose control of bodily functions.
500	18	Coma, parts of brain controlling breathing and heartbeat can shut down. Likely to die without medical assistance.

Long-term effects

Large amounts of alcohol taken over a long period of time can cause a lot of damage to the body. A young drinker will not be harmed in the long term, however, if they stop drinking or drink sensibly.

Effects on the body

These are the changes to the main organs when a person drinks alcohol:

• Heart – alcohol increases the heart rate, which speeds up the blood flow around the body. This can cause problems with blood pressure.

• Liver – the liver breaks down and removes alcohol from the body. This process takes time and the liver can only cope with 15 mg of alcohol every hour. In the long term, if someone drinks a lot of alcohol every day, the liver never gets a break and will eventually be permanently damaged.

← After a night of heavy drinking you are likely to have a hangover the next day.

← These men are heavy drinkers. Many people who drink too much look older than they actually are.

• Stomach – drinking too much alcohol can cause ulcers, which can stop someone being able to eat properly.

• Brain – the brain is affected by alcohol very quickly. How it is affected depends on how much alcohol a person has had to drink. Eating while drinking alcohol can slow down the effects on the brain. In the long term, drinking too much can cause sleeplessness, loss of memory and anxiety.

FACT

Pregnant women who drink risk having babies with defects. The most serious defects include mental-health problems, growth deficiency, head and facial deformities, joint and limb abnormalities, and heart defects.

FACTS ABOUT ALCOHOL, ADDICTION RESEARCH FOUNDATION, TORONTO, CANADA.

How much is it safe to drink?

Alcohol is measured in units. Each type of alcohol contains a certain number of units. For example, half a pint of cider or a single shot of spirit contains one unit.

Scientists have studied how alcohol affects our health and how many units are safe to drink. Recent research has suggested that small amounts of alcohol may protect a person against heart disease, but other experts say that people should not be told that alcohol is good for them, even if it is just small amounts.

⬇ Alcohol and violence often go together. Here, Turkish and English football fans are fighting.

Alcohol and violence

Another problem with alcohol is that drinking too much often leads to violence. Sometimes people drink when watching sports, and fights can break out between supporters of different teams. If people drink a lot it can lead to violence in the home. The important thing about drinking is knowing your own limitations and understanding when to stop.

CASE STUDY ▸ CASE STUDY ▸

Paul had his eighteenth birthday party coming up. He wanted to celebrate with his friends but he knew his mum and dad would be worried about everyone getting drunk. They were scared that it would be like his older brother's party, when the police were called by neighbours. Paul decided to talk it through with his parents. They had gone away for his brother's party so they all decided it would be better if they were around for Paul's party. After talking it through, they planned a family party with a DJ for the young people. They decided there would be some alcohol but also lots of food and non-alcoholic drinks. Paul was really happy with how the party went. Everybody had a good time and the police weren't called!

⬇ Many young men don't think they can have a good time without alcohol.

Different people, different effects

'My first experience of really drinking alcohol was when my uncle brought a crate of beer to a party. I had five or six bottles. I didn't really have too many problems but I remember being very loud and people told me what embarrassing things I had said while I was drunk. I felt fine the next day.'
PAUL, 15

'Last summer holidays we were at a party and I got so drunk that I climbed up on to the roof of a building. I lost my balance and ended up falling off – I really hurt myself. Then I was violently sick. I felt awful the next day. It's really put me off drinking alcohol.'
MARCUS, 14

The effects of alcohol depend on several things:

• How much alcohol has been drunk.

• Whether the drink is mixed with other drinks.

• The drinker's height, weight and sex.

• How much food is in the stomach.

• The drinker's mood.

• Current state of health.

⬇ This man is used to drinking neat spirits. Most people would become very drunk and possibly seriously ill if they drank like this.

Sensible drinking

General guidelines for sensible drinking suggest that women should not drink more than 14 units of alcohol per week and that men should not drink more than 21 units of alcohol per week.

Young people, who usually weigh less and are not as used to alcohol as most adults, should drink fewer units than the guidelines above suggest.

⬇ Physically, women are less able to deal with alcohol, so the effects can be greater.

Why do people drink alcohol?

Most people drink alcohol because it helps them enjoy themselves. It makes them feel relaxed and more confident. Many people think that the positive effects of drinking outweigh the negative effects.

'When I want to celebrate something really important, such as a birthday, I like Champagne. At home, after work, I might have a glass of wine because I like the taste. They say it's good for you!'
LEE, 27

⬇ Lewis Hamilton and Nico Rosberg celebrate with Champagne after the Australian Grand Prix in 2008.

Reasons why people may drink:

- To relax and relieve stress after a busy day.

- To feel at ease when meeting new people.

- To celebrate anything from a wedding, a christening or a birthday, to winning at sport.

- To complement food – as well as adding flavour, people like to drink alcohol with a meal.

- For health reasons – some medical research shows that a small amount of alcohol can be good for you.

- It is easily available – alcohol can often be bought in supermarkets and corner shops.

- It becomes a habit – alcohol can be addictive.

⬆ A toast with Champagne to celebrate a birthday party.

Young drinkers

Alcohol is readily available, so many young people can get hold of it. Most people also keep some alcohol at home, and this is where many young people have their first taste of it. In this situation, either their parents give them alcohol, or they try it secretly.

Other reasons young people decide to drink include:

• To get the buzz – alcohol can be exciting and fun.

• To fit in with the crowd.

• To feel popular and less nervous in social situations.

• To forget problems at home.

• Out of boredom – drinking is something to do.

• Drinking seems exciting and grown-up.

⬆ For some young people, sport is a good way to keep fit and avoid drinking too much alcohol.

Feeling like an adult

Many young people think drinking alcohol makes them seem more adult. Boys may feel that drinking large amounts is grown up. Girls may drink alcohol to show they can keep up with the boys. Research suggests that young people are drinking from a younger age and drinking more.

⬇ Some young people are tempted to drink too much because their friends are doing the same.

FACT

Binge drinking is defined as a man having five or more drinks in a row, or a woman having four or more drinks. Although college students commonly binge drink, 70 per cent of binge-drinking episodes involve adults over the age of 25.

CENTERS FOR DISEASE CONTROL AND PREVENTION, 2009.

Alcohol and the media

⬆ Images used in advertising often show the glamorous side of drinking alcohol.

Even though alcohol is a drug, most people find it socially acceptable. As a result, alcohol regularly appears in the media. Films and television programmes often show people drinking alcohol and having fun. Television commercials show similar images.

FACT

Research on responses to alcohol advertising on television showed that the more boys aged 14 to 17 liked the advertisements, the more likely they were to be drinkers, to have higher annual consumption (about 67 cans over the past year), and to expect to drink more frequently in the future.

LINDA HILL, 'YOUNG PEOPLE AND ALCOHOL, CHILD TO ADULT: THE DUNEDIN STUDY'.

CASE STUDY ▸ CASE STUDY ▸ CASE STUDY ▸ CASE STUDY ▸

Paul always watched a lot of films and television. He particularly liked action films and there were always cool people drinking beer. 'It was always in my face, I just couldn't get away from it,' he said. One night, when Paul was 11 and his parents were out, he and a group of friends found a crate of lager in the garage and decided to drink it for a laugh. It was really good fun to start with – the beer didn't taste very nice but it made everyone giggle. They drank more and more, and enjoyed dancing and messing about. Paul suddenly felt giddy though. He was sick on the carpet and passed out. The next morning he felt terrible and told himself he'd never drink again.

Advertising alcohol

Some people argue that alcohol is as bad for you as smoking. Tobacco advertising is banned, but advertisements for alcohol are still allowed on television, in magazines and on billboards. The people who make alcohol know that most people think drinking is fun. They make advertisements that show people enjoying alcohol in exotic locations or in exciting situations.

➡ Some films seem to glamorize drinking alcohol. In the film *Cocktail*, Tom Cruise plays a hip young barman.

What are the problems with alcohol?

Most people do not have problems with alcohol. However, as more and more people start drinking, the problems associated with alcohol increase, too.

Dangerous driving

Drinking and driving is one of the worst alcohol-related problems. Young people who drink are five times more likely to have an accident than non-drinkers. In the USA, a woman whose 13-year-old daughter was killed by a drunk driver started MADD (Mothers Against Drunk Driving), which campaigns for stricter laws against drinking and driving.

➡ The risk of a car accident is higher when a person has been drinking.

The social effects of alcohol

Every year, all over the world, many work days are lost due to people being off sick with hangovers or other alcohol-related problems. This has a big effect on many businesses.

The cost to health services for alcohol-related illnesses is also growing. Alcohol not only causes physical health problems, it can cause mental health problems, such as depression.

Some crimes are also related to alcohol abuse. Domestic violence and child abuse while under the influence of alcohol are increasing.

⬆ An anti-drinking sign painted by children in Sri Lanka is a sad reminder of the problems with alcohol.

'The majority of our patients come in with problems that are related to alcohol in some way or another. You have fights, car crashes and accidents and then there is the illness, all of which are caused by too much alcohol over many years.'
NURSE, UK

What is alcohol dependency?

It is important to remember that alcohol is a drug, so there is a danger that someone may become addicted to it. Some people become physically dependent on alcohol, which means that their bodies do not work properly and they feel ill without drinking alcohol.

FACT

Many famous people have been drink-dependent or had parents who were dependent on alcohol. Ludwig van Beethoven (1770-1827), the famous German composer, had a drink-dependent father. As a result, Beethoven had to go out to work at an early age. Elvis Presley (1935-1977), the singer and actor, died aged just 42 of what is thought to have been drug and alcohol abuse.

← Elvis Presley in 1971, just six years before he died. Here he is starting to look ill from years of alcohol and drug abuse.

Who becomes alcohol dependent?

It is easy to think that people who are dependent on alcohol are loners or homeless. In fact, many people who drink come from nice homes and have good jobs. These people find it difficult to admit they have a problem with alcohol. They may not seem to get particularly drunk, but they need to drink alcohol to cope with their lives.

⬇ Alcohol dependency can mean drinking anything with alcohol in it. These South Africans are drinking a deadly mixture of beer and car battery fluid.

How do people become drink-dependent?

It is not easy to say why one person becomes dependent on alcohol and another does not. Some people cope better with stress than others. Some people have more difficult jobs and family lives than others.

Something may have happened to make a person feel lonely or depressed, so they turn to alcohol to forget their problems. Some people start drinking because they are bored, but they keep drinking because it becomes a habit.

FACT

Those children who had tried alcohol at age nine were more likely than others to have experienced alcohol-related problems by age 18.

LINDA HILL, YOUNG PEOPLE AND ALCOHOL.

← Losing a husband or wife can cause someone to start drinking heavily.

CASE STUDY ▸ CASE STUDY ▸ CASE STUDY ▸ CASE STUDY ▸

Gail had been friends with Sarah for many years. Gail had noticed at times that Sarah's behaviour was strange, secretive and, once or twice, she had even lied about certain things. It never occurred to Gail that Sarah was an alcoholic. Sarah was a nurse and held a very responsible position in the hospital where she worked. She was kind and thoughtful. One day, Sarah admitted herself to a special unit for treating people with alcohol problems. She told Gail she had been drinking heavily since she was 14 years old.

Problems in later life

As people are starting to drink at a younger age, governments around the world are concerned that there will be a rise in the number of people who become alcohol dependent.

To address the problem, governments are introducing laws such as minimum-age laws. They are also making punishments stricter for people who break the laws.

➡ When the pressures of work and family life get too much, alcohol can seem the answer for some people.

Getting help

There are many places that offer help, advice and treatment for people who are alcohol-dependent. Admitting that they have a problem in the first place is the most important step on the road to recovery.

Drying out

People with alcohol problems may be treated in hospitals or special clinics. They can also get help at support meetings or counselling sessions. Giving up alcohol, or 'drying out', can be long and difficult. People may need medicine to help with the withdrawal symptoms. They might need treatment for other conditions related to drinking.

⬇ Counselling is an important part of recovering from alcohol dependency.

'I drank just to get rid of my feeling of not being wanted or really loved. It took me a broken marriage and nearly losing my job before I would admit that I needed help.'
SHAUN, 40, WHO STARTED DRINKING AT THE AGE OF 12

Living in sobriety

Many people who are dependent on alcohol must learn how to never drink again. This is called living in sobriety. Some recovering dependent drinkers join an organization called Alcoholics Anonymous (AA). This is made up of local groups of recovering drinkers or ex-drinkers, who provide support for each other.

Overcoming dependency

Many people think that once someone is dependent on alcohol they are dependent for life. It is not easy to recover from an alcohol addiction, but with the help of organizations like the AA, it is possible to overcome a dependency.

➡ Help can be just a phone call away, but admitting there is a problem has to come first.

Making choices

People's opinions about alcohol usually depend on their own experiences of it. If someone has an alcoholic in their family, they may have seen the damage it can causes to other people. If someone works as a nurse or a paramedic, they see people every day whose lives are affected by alcohol.

⬇ Drinking alcohol isn't always fun. This girl has just been sick and needs her friend's help.

Personal experience

A young person who gets drunk for the first time and has fun might think that drinking alcohol is exciting. They will probably drink again.

A young person who gets drunk for the first time and is sick would probably have a very different opinion.

'A lot of the time with our work, alcohol has been involved in some way or another. I drink, but having seen all the problems caused by alcohol, I drink in moderation.'

AMBULANCE DRIVER, NEW YORK, USA

'Friday and Saturday night fights are triggered by people just not knowing when to stop drinking. This leads to arguments which end up in a big fight. This isn't just in the pubs and clubs but also in people's homes.'

POLICEMAN, BIRMINGHAM, UK

'It's OK if you drink a little bit of alcohol and become merry. But if you drink a lot and become drunk it is not very nice for people around you.'

JULIAN, 13, LILLE, FRANCE

'Come off it! A party with no booze? You've got to be joking.'

MICHAEL, 21, MANCHESTER, UK

'I like my glass of wine after a long day at work.'

JANETTE, 31, ILLINOIS, USA

➡ Many people can enjoy a drink without becoming alcoholics.

Decide for yourself

Everyone has choices to make about alcohol when they get older:

• You must decide whether you want to drink or not.

• You will be in control of how much you drink.

• You can encourage your friends to drink or you can respect their choices.

• You will know when you are over the legal limit and you can say 'no' at any time.

⬆ If you do drink alcohol, only you can decide how much is right for you to drink.

CASE STUDY ▸ CASE STUDY ▸ CASE STUDY ▸ CASE STUDY ▸

When Kathy was 15 she saw drinking alcohol as part of growing up. If she could show everyone how much she could drink then her mates would look up to her. One day she made a bet with Jo, her best friend. They bet on who could drink the most. They started drinking some lager and then, when they ran out, they stole vodka from Kathy's parents' drink cabinet. Both girls drank until they passed out. Fortunately, Kathy's mother found them and called an ambulance. They both ended up in hospital with alcohol poisoning.

FACT

A survey of young people aged 15 to 16 found that many of them experience problems due to the misuse of alcohol. On average, 21 per cent of teenagers reported individual problems, such as reduced performance at school. 22 per cent reported relationship problems and 12 per cent reported delinquency problems, such as violence and fighting.

ESPAD REPORT,
CAN AND COUNCIL OF EUROPE.

Units of alcohol

- 1 glass of wine = 1 unit

- ½ pint of beer/lager = 1 unit

- 1 can of strong lager = 3 units

- ½ bottle of vodka = 15 units

⬇ After working all week, these young Zambian men enjoy a few beers on a Friday night to relax.

Tips for sensible drinking

Most adults try to drink responsibly in the following ways:

• They have food with alcohol. This stops the alcohol being absorbed so quickly.

• They may have a non-alcoholic drink in between each alcoholic one.

• They think about what they are drinking – the higher the alcohol content, the more quickly it is absorbed into the body.

• They do not mix different types of alcohol.

• They understand that spirits mixed with a soft drink may taste less alcoholic, but they still have a high alcohol content.

• They may drink only at weekends or on special occasions.

• They plan how much they are going to drink before they go out.

⬇ Drinking orange juice between each alcoholic drink is this girl's way of making sure she doesn't get too drunk.

• If a friend says they do not want another drink, they do not pressurize them into having one.

• They firmly say 'No!' if someone tries to make them have another drink and they do not want to.

Alcohol is part of our society and it is here to stay. It can be consumed safely, and in a fun way, without harming your health. It's up to you.

⬆ Alcohol is just one way of having fun. There are many other things to give you a buzz.

'One thing I know about alcohol is that it can be very dangerous and that it is not good to drink too much of it. You can become addicted to it and it can make you do things you do not want to do. It is okay to have a little bit of alcohol but not too much.'
KATY, 14

GLOSSARY

Addiction

When a person cannot stop doing something, even when it is harmful.

Alcoholic

A person who is addicted to drinking alcohol.

Binge drinking

When a person drinks one alcoholic drink after another, very quickly.

Bootleggers

People who illegally smuggled alcohol into the USA during the period of Prohibition.

Breweries

Buildings where beer or lager is usually produced.

Delinquency

Minor crimes, usually committed by young people.

Dependency

When a person has to have something to help them cope.

Depressant drug

A drug that causes the body to slow down. Alcohol is a depressant drug.

Distillation

The process of evaporating or boiling a liquid to make it more concentrated or purer.

Domestic violence

When a person hits out at and hurts the person they are married to or live with. Often people become violent as a result of drinking too much.

Drying out

When somebody who drinks too much stops drinking.

Fermentation

A chemical reaction in which yeast breaks down the sugar in fruit, for example, and changes it to alcohol.

Fined

Having to pay money as a punishment for a crime.

Hangover

The after-effects of drinking too much alcohol. Effects include headaches, tiredness and sickness.

Legal

Something that people are permitted to do by law.

Licence

Permission from an authority to allow pubs, restaurants, wine bars, etc., to sell alcohol.

Long term

Something that happens over a long period of time.

Measure

A certain quantity of something.

Minimum legal age

The youngest age at which you are allowed to do something.

Moderate drinking

Drinking amounts of alcohol that do not exceed the recommended weekly amounts, i.e. 14 units for women and 21 units for men.

Prohibit

To stop something from happening.

Sobriety

When a person does not get drunk from alcohol. We often say that a person lives in sobriety if they do not drink.

Under-age drinking

Drinking alcohol below the legal age for drinking.

Withdrawal symptoms

How the body reacts when a drug that someone has become dependent on is no longer taken.

FURTHER INFORMATION

ORGANIZATIONS

Worldwide there are organizations providing information and advice about alcohol. The organizations below can supply educational material and resources.

UK

Alcoholics Anonymous
PO Box 1
10 Toft Green
York, YO1 7NJ
National helpline: 0845 769 7555
www.alcoholics-
anonymous.org.uk/

Alcohol Concern
64 Leman Street
London, E1 8EU
Tel: 020 7264 0510
www.alcoholconcern.org.uk

Al-anon Family Groups
61 Great Dover Street
London, SE1 4YF
24-hour helpline: 020 7403 0888
www.al-anonuk.org.uk

National Institute for Health and Clinical Excellency (NICE)
MidCity Place, 71 High Holborn
London WC1V 6NA
Tel: 0845 003 7780
www.nice.org.uk

Tacade
Old Exchange Buildings
6 St Ann's Passage
King Street
Manchester M2 6AD
Tel: 0161 836 6850
www.tacade.com

USA

Alcoholics Anonymous
PO Box 459
Grand Central Station
New York, 10163
Tel: (212) 870 3400
www.aa.org

NCADD (National Council on Alcoholism and Drug Dependence)
12 West 21 Street
New York 10010
Tel: (212) 206 6770
www.ncadd.org

Useful telephone numbers
Drinkline
Tel: 0800 917 8282
Gives confidential support and advice. Will put you in touch with your local alcohol advice centre.

National Drugs Helpline
(Talk to Frank)
Tel: 0800 77 66 00
www.talktofrank.com

FURTHER READING

Talk About: Drugs
by Jacqui Bailey
(Wayland, 2008)

Know the Facts: Drinking and Smoking
by Paul Mason
(Wayland, 2008)

Healthy Body: Drink, Drugs and Your Body
by Polly Goodman
(Wayland, 2005)

INDEX